- You can return this item to any Bournemouth library but not all libraries are open every day.

- Items must be returned on or before the due date. Please note that you will be charged for items returned late.

- Items may be renewed unless requested by another customer.

- Renewals can be made in any library, by telephone, email or online via the website. Your membership card number and PIN will be required.

- Please look after this item - you may be charged for any damage.

www.bournemouth.gov.uk/libraries

Raintree is an imprint of Capstone Global Library Limited, a company incorporated in England and Wales having its registered office at 264 Banbury Road, Oxford, OX2 7DY – Registered company number: 6695582

www.raintree.co.uk
myorders@raintree.co.uk

Edited by Sarah L Schuette
Designed by Jennifer Bergstrom
Picture research by Kelly Garvin
Originated by Capstone Global Library Ltd
Printed and bound in India.

ISBN 978 1 4747 3549 0 (hardback)
20 19 18 17 16
10 9 8 7 6 5 4 3 2 1

ISBN 978 1 4747 3554 4 (paperback)
21 20 19 18 17
10 9 8 7 6 5 4 3 2 1

British Library Cataloguing in Publication Data
A full catalogue record for this book is available from the British Library.

Acknowledgements
We would like to thank the following for permission to reproduce photographs:
Capstone Studio: Karon Dubke, cover; Shutterstock: Aleksey Stemmer, (sun flowers) 22, Angel DiBilio, 13, Anna Moskvina, 11, Balakirev Vladimir, 1, Bildagentur Zoonar GmbH, 7, Bogdan Wankowicz, (seed) 22, janaph, 19, Olga Prolygina, 15, SusaZoom, 21, Thanamat Somwan, 17, vandame, 5, Varina Patel, 9

We would like to thank Judson R Scott, past President of American Society of Consulting Arborists for his invaluable help in the preparation of this book.

Contents

Plants need flowers

Flowers make seeds
and fruit for plants.
Flowers come in many
colours, shapes and sizes.

Flower buds grow
from the stem of a plant.
The buds open
and flowers bloom.

Flowers have pollen inside.

Pollen helps flowers
make seeds.

Parts of the flower
turn into fruit.

Seeds grow inside the fruit.

New plants grow from seeds.

All kinds of flowers

Colourful flower petals
attract birds.
The birds sip on nectar
inside the flowers.

Roses have soft petals
that smell good.
Roses grow on bushes.

Flowers we eat

We eat some flowers.

Cauliflower is a white flower.

We eat it raw or cooked.

Artichokes are flower buds.

They make good dips

and sauces.

Wonderful flowers

Pretty or plain,
large or small,
flowers help plants
make fruit and seeds.

Parts of a sunflower

flower

stem

leaves

seed

root

Glossary

attract   be interested or drawn closer to something

bud   small shoot on a plant that grows into a flower or a leaf; buds grow from plant stems

nectar   sweet liquid inside flowers

pollen   tiny yellow grains made in flowers

seed   part of a flowering plant that can grow into a new plant

stem   long main part of a plant that makes leaves

Find out more

All About Flowers (All About Plants), Claire Throp (Raintree, 2015)

All About Plants (Ways Into Science), Peter Riley (Franklin Watts, 2016)

Flowers (My First Book of Nature), Victoria Munson (Wayland, 2017)

Index

Websites

http://activityvillage.co.uk/flowers
Enjoy many different crafts and activities all about flowers!

http://www.sciencekids.co.nz/sciencefacts/plants.html
Fun facts about all different types of plants and flowers.